Author Biographies

Dr. Seuss

Charlotte Guillain

Heinemann Library
Chicago, Illinois

H **www.capstonepub.com**
Visit our website to find out
more information about
Heinemann-Raintree books.

To order:

☎ Phone 800-747-4992

🖥 Visit www.capstonepub.com
to browse our catalog and order online.

Edited by Rebecca Rissman, Daniel Nunn, and
Sian Smith
Designed by Joanna Hinton-Malivoire
Picture research by Tracy Cummins
Production by Victoria Fitzgerald
Originated by Capstone Global Library Ltd
Printed in the United States of America in North
Mankato, Minnesota.   112015   009332RP

17 16 15
11 10 9 8

**Library of Congress Cataloging-in-Publication
Data**

Guillain, Charlotte.
Dr. Seuss / Charlotte Guillain.
p.cm.—(Author biographies)
Includes bibliographical references and index.
ISBN 978-1-4329-5959-3 (hardback)
ISBN 978-1-4329-5965-4 (paperback)
1. Seuss, Dr.—Juvenile literature. 2. Authors,
American—20th century—Biography—Juvenile
literature. 3. Illustrators—United States—Biography—
Juvenile literature. 4. Children's literature—
Authorship—Juvenile literature. I. Title.
  PS3513.E2Z686 2012
  813'.52—dc22   2011016060
  [B]

Acknowledgments

We would like to thank the following for permission
to reproduce photographs: Alamy Images pp. 17,
22c (© Everett Collection Inc), 21, 22e (© Randy
Duchaine); AP Photo pp. 9, 11 (Roswell Daily Record,
Andrew Poertner), 14, 22d; Corbis pp. 4 (© James
L. Amos), 13 (© KEVIN LAMARQUE/Reuters); Getty
Images pp. 5, 10 (John Bryson/Time Life Pictures),
12, 16, 18 (Gene Lester); The Kobal Collection pp. 19
(MGM TV), 20, 22b (BLUE SKY/20TH CENTURY FOX);
Library of Congress Prints and Photographs Division
p. 6; Newscom p. 15 (HO/AFP/GETTY IMAGES);
Museum of Springfield History pp. 7, 8 (Seuss
Museum); Shutterstock p. 22a (© Supri Saharjoto).

Cover photograph of Theodor Seuss Geisel shaking
hands with Cat in the Hat in 1988 reproduced
with permission of AP Photo (Burt Steel). Back
cover image of Springfield, Massachusetts in 1908
reproduced with permission of Library of Congress
Prints and Photographs Division.

Every effort has been made to contact copyright
holders of material reproduced in this book. Any
omissions will be rectified in subsequent printings if
notice is given to the publisher.

Contents

Some words are shown in bold, **like this**. You can find them in the glossary on page 23.

Who Was Dr. Seuss?

Dr. Seuss was a writer.

He wrote and **illustrated** stories for children.

His real name was Theodor Seuss Geisel, and he wasn't really a doctor!

His most famous book is *The Cat in the Hat.*

Where Did He Grow Up?

Dr. Seuss was born in 1904.

He grew up in the city of Springfield, Massachusetts.

His family had moved to the United States from Germany.

His family and friends called him Ted.

What Did He Do Before He Was a Writer?

Dr. Seuss studied in the United States and England.

He started drawing cartoons when he was a student.

He got a job drawing cartoons for magazines.

Then he started drawing **advertisements**.

How Did He Start Writing Books?

Dr. Seuss's job didn't let him write books for adults.

But he was allowed to write children's books.

He wrote an ABC book but nobody would **publish** it.

But then he went on to write many popular books for children.

What Books Did He Write?

Dr. Seuss's best-known book is *The Cat in the Hat.*

It is about a talking cat who visits some children on a rainy day.

Green Eggs and Ham is another favorite for many readers.

The book is about how it can be good to try new things.

What Did He Write About?

Dr. Seuss's books are very funny.

The words in his stories usually rhyme.

USA 37

THEODOR SEUSS GEISEL

2004

His books are full of strange animals and places.

He often makes readers think about how to do the right thing.

What Are the Pictures Like in Dr. Seuss's Books?

Dr. Seuss's pictures are in a cartoon style.

He drew his pictures using pen and ink.

Some of his pictures are black and white or only use a few colors.

In his later books he used more color.

What Else Did He Like to Do?

Dr. Seuss was also an artist.

He produced many paintings and **sculptures**.

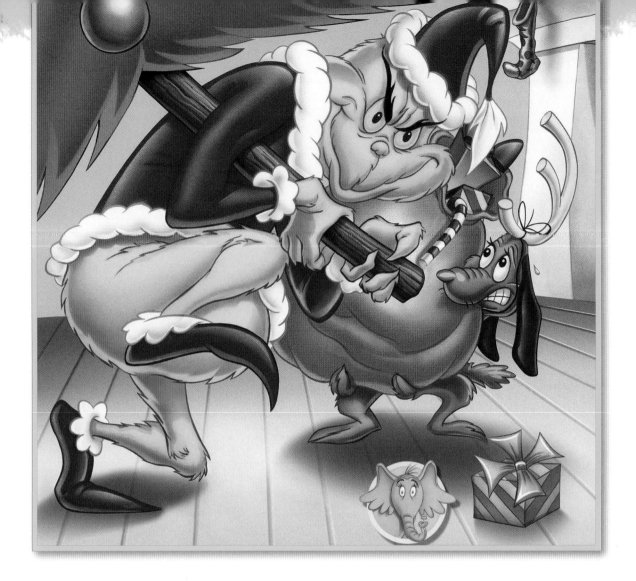

He made movies when he was a
young man.

Later he helped to make movies of his
stories for television.

Why Is He Famous Today?

People still buy Dr. Seuss's books today.

His books have been made into movies, cartoons, and plays.

People can visit the Dr. Seuss National Memorial Sculpture Garden in Springfield.

There are statues of Dr. Seuss and many of his **characters** there.

Timeline of Dr. Seuss's Life and Work

1904   Dr. Seuss was born.

1925   Dr. Seuss's first cartoon was **published**.

1937   Dr. Seuss's first book, *And to Think That I Saw It on Mulberry Street,* was published.

1957   *The Cat in the Hat* and *How the Grinch Stole Christmas!* were published.

1990   Dr. Seuss's last book, *Oh the Places You'll Go!,* was published.

1991   Dr. Seuss died.

2002   The Dr. Seuss National Memorial Sculpture Garden opened.

Glossary

 **advertisement** a picture or short commercial used to tell people about things they could buy

 **character** person or animal in a story

 **illustrate** draw or paint pictures to go with a story

 **publish** make into a book and have the book printed

 **sculpture** model that an artist makes, such as a statue

Find Out More

Books

Some of Dr. Seuss's books: *The Cat in the Hat, The Cat in the Hat Comes Back, Green Eggs and Ham, How the Grinch Stole Christmas!, One Fish, Two Fish, Red Fish, Blue Fish, The Lorax*, and *Oh, the Places You'll Go!*

Websites

www.seussville.com
Visit the official Dr. Seuss website to find out more about the writer and his books, watch videos, and play games.

Index